American ✩ CULTURE & CONFLICT

Living Through WORLD WAR I

M. M. Eboch

Educational Media

rourkeeducationalmedia.com

Before Reading:

Building Academic Vocabulary and Background Knowledge

Before reading a book, it is important to tap into what your child or students already know about the topic. This will help them develop their vocabulary, increase their reading comprehension, and make connections across the curriculum.

1. *Look at the cover of the book. What will this book be about?*
2. *What do you already know about the topic?*
3. *Let's study the Table of Contents. What will you learn about in the book's chapters?*
4. *What would you like to learn about this topic? Do you think you might learn about it from this book? Why or why not?*
5. *Use a reading journal to write about your knowledge of this topic. Record what you already know about the topic and what you hope to learn about the topic.*
6. *Read the book.*
7. *In your reading journal, record what you learned about the topic and your response to the book.*
8. *After reading the book complete the activities below.*

Content Area Vocabulary

Read the list. What do these words mean?

combat

discrimination

economy

intolerance

neutral

pacifists

patriotic

philanthropists

segregated

treaty

troops

After Reading:

Comprehension and Extension Activity

After reading the book, work on the following questions with your child or students in order to check their level of reading comprehension and content mastery.

1. *How did the death of an Austrian couple lead to countries around the world going to war? (Summarize)*
2. *Why did the need for soldiers open new jobs for women and African Americans? (Infer)*
3. *How did the Great Migration change the country? (Asking Questions)*
4. *How involved in other countries' affairs do you think the United States should be? (Text to Self Connection)*
5. *How did World War I help improve medicine? (Asking Questions)*

Extension Activity

Look at some American posters from World War I. What effects might the posters have had on the American people? How did this help the war effort? How did it increase intolerance in America? Design your own poster to encourage people to support the war effort. Can you do so without encouraging hatred?

TABLE OF CONTENTS

KEY EVENTS

June 28, 1914:	Archduke Franz Ferdinand and his wife, Sophie, are assassinated by Gavrilo Princip
July 28, 1914:	Austria-Hungary declares war on Serbia
August 1914:	More European countries join the war The United States remains neutral
April 6, 1917:	The United States declares war on Germany
June 5, 1917:	The U.S. draft for military service opens
June 1917:	The first U.S. troops arrive in Europe
November 11, 1918:	Germany surrenders
June 28, 1919:	A peace treaty officially ends the war with Germany
August 10, 1920:	The Allies and the Ottoman Empire sign a peace treaty

CHAPTER ONE

A WORLD AT WAR

Gavrilo Princip (1894 - 1918) killed the Austrian prince and his wife.

The "War to End All Wars" began with one person. In 1914, a young man from Serbia plotted violence. He wanted to end the rule of Austria-Hungary over his country. He shot and killed an Austrian prince and his wife.

A WAR TO END ALL WARS?

We now call the conflict from 1914 -1918 the First World War or World War I. At the time, no one knew another world war would follow. Then the conflict was known as the Great War, or the War to End All Wars.

Art in an Italian paper shows the murder of Archduke Franz Ferdinand and his wife, Sophie, which started World War I.

This led to more change than the young Serb could have imagined. On July 28, Austria-Hungary declared war on Serbia. Germany supported Austria-Hungary. Russia, Belgium, France, and Great Britain backed Serbia. The Great War had begun.

A city in Poland shows damage from the war.

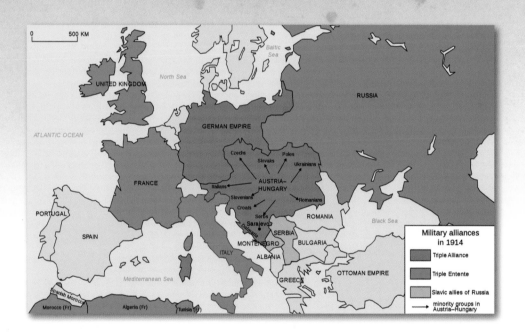

THE POWERS OF WAR

Over time, other countries joined each side of the conflict. Germany, Austria-Hungary, Bulgaria, and the Ottoman Empire fought on one side. They are known as the Central Powers. Great Britain, France, Russia, Italy, Romania, Japan, and the United States fought on the other side. They are known as the Allied Powers or Allies.

In Washington's Farewell Address, he said the U. S. should not get involved in other countries' affairs.

A painting of George Washington, America's first president.

George Washington (1732 -1799) had warned the United States against becoming involved in European wars. America followed this isolationist policy for 150 years. Isolationism means staying out of the affairs of other countries.

As war raged in Europe, the U.S. stayed **neutral**. Businesses wanted to be able to trade with every country in Europe. Americans wanted to avoid the horrors of war. German Americans especially did not want their new country to fight with their old one.

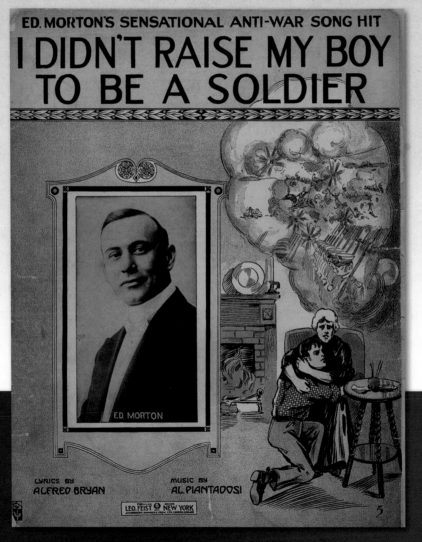

ED. MORTON'S SENSATIONAL ANTI-WAR SONG HIT

I DIDN'T RAISE MY BOY TO BE A SOLDIER

E.D. MORTON

LYRICS BY
ALFRED BRYAN

MUSIC BY
AL. PIANTADOSI

LEO. FEIST NEW YORK

NO SOLDIER

Music often reflects what is happening in the world. In 1915, the song "I Didn't Raise My Boy to Be a Soldier" was a hit. It reached the top of the American music charts.

German submarines like the one on the right sometimes captured or sunk ships.

A German submarine, also known as a U-boat.

Americans could not ignore the war forever. The Germans wanted to block supplies from getting to Britain. They used submarines to attack supply ships. Americans sometimes traveled on these ships. In 1915, the Germans sunk the British ship Lusitania, killing nearly 1,200 people. Among them were 128 Americans. U.S. public opinion turned against Germany.

Some people claimed the U.S. needed to build up a strong military for defense. A Preparedness Movement suggested the country prepare for war—just in case. People across America began to get ready. However, most Americans still thought the country should stay out of the war.

A painting shows the 1915 sinking of the Lusitania.

THE AMERICAN WAR–DOG

(The American-German crisis, January–March, 1916)

A political cartoon shows President Wilson looking out his door. The howling dog represents Americans who want to join the Great War.

Opening game 1916. Rx 112

After winning reelection, President Wilson threw out the first pitch at a baseball game.

NO WAR!

American President Woodrow Wilson (1856-1924) ran for reelection in 1916. His campaign claimed that "He kept us out of war." An ad said, "You are working, not fighting; alive and happy, not cannon fodder." Cannon fodder meant soldiers sent into battle to die. The promise to avoid war helped Wilson win the election.

CHAPTER TWO

AMERICA JOINS THE WAR

German submarines sank more ships, including U.S. ships. Many Americans died. Then America heard about a secret message. Germany had offered U.S. territory to Mexico if Mexico would join Germany.

A man buys a paper from a newsboy. The headline reads, "U.S. at War with Germany."

Outraged Americans changed their opinions about the war. It had now become personal. Newspapers published both accurate news and rumors. Many stories portrayed Germany as a vicious enemy.

German submarines in port.

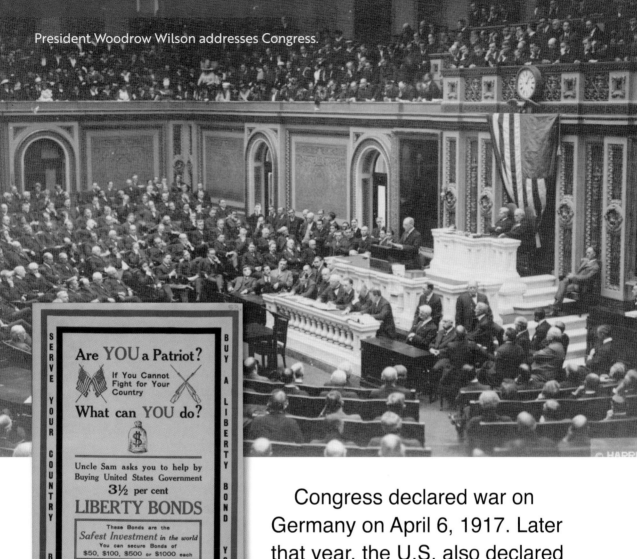

President Woodrow Wilson addresses Congress.

Are YOU a Patriot?

If You Cannot
Fight for Your
Country

What can YOU do?

Uncle Sam asks you to help by
Buying United States Government

3½ per cent

LIBERTY BONDS

These Bonds are the
Safest Investment in the world
You can secure Bonds of
$50, $100, $500 or $1000 each

Buy your Bonds through your Boss or
your Bank, who will act without charge

If you do not have all the cash
join the

Liberty Loan Club

In which
$1.00 a week for 50 weeks buys a $50 Bond
2.00 "   "   "   "   " 100 "
10.00 "   "   "   "   " 500 "
20.00 "   "   "   "   " 1000 "

Consult Your Nearest Bank

An ad for Liberty Bonds asks, "Are YOU a Patriot?"

Congress declared war on Germany on April 6, 1917. Later that year, the U.S. also declared war on Austria-Hungary.

CHANGE OF MIND

President Wilson had to provide good reasons for changing his opinion on going to war. "The world must be made safe for democracy," he claimed. He called Germany's submarine attacks "a war against mankind. It is a war against all nations."

The U.S. Secretary of War drew the first draft number while blindfolded. The names drawn would be called to serve in the military.

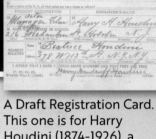

A Draft Registration Card. This one is for Harry Houdini (1874-1926), a famous magician.

Patriotic fever spread across America. Now the public supported the war with enthusiasm. But only 73,000 men volunteered for the Army. The U.S. military would need far more soldiers.

An ad for the military encourages people to volunteer.

The new Selective Service Act allowed the government to draft soldiers. At first, only men between the ages of 21 and 30 could be drafted. Soon the age range was expanded. Men from ages 18 to 45 could be drafted as soldiers. Nearly 5 million Americans would serve in World War I. About 1.4 million would fight in active **combat**.

Young men in New York City register for the draft in 1917.

THE DRAFT THEN AND NOW

In earlier times, each American colony or state had its own draft. People could hire substitutes or pay money to avoid service. The Selective Service Act stopped those practices. Men can still avoid the draft under certain conditions, such as health problems. If they are opposed to war for religious or moral reasons, they can avoid combat jobs.

The U.S. government needed Americans to support the war movement. The Committee on Public Information got to work. This government organization tried to influence public opinion. Posters showed Germans carrying off helpless young women. Many American men became so angry they were willing to go to war to kill Germans.

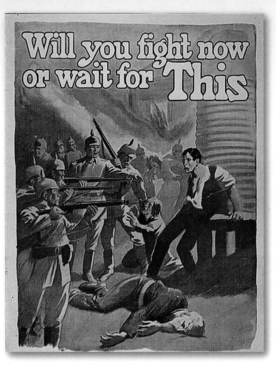

A poster uses dramatic images to encourage people to fight Germany.

Hollywood supported the pro-war and anti-German feelings. Movies were released with titles such as *To Hell with the Kaiser* and *The Kaiser, the Beast of Berlin*. They encouraged enthusiasm about fighting the enemy.

DO NOT RESIST

*The U.S. government tried to keep anyone from hurting the war effort. This included passing laws designed to control people. The Sedition Act made it illegal to insult the U.S. government, the flag, the military, or the Constitution. This and other laws targeted **pacifists** and others opposed to the war.*

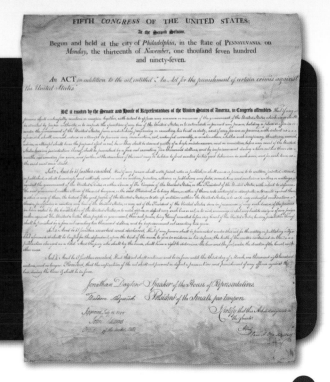

Many German immigrants and descendents of Germans lived in America. The hate against Germany turned toward them as well. Americans burned German books and banned the playing of German music. Schools stopped teaching German. Some German Americans were imprisoned or killed simply for their German blood.

Other groups also suffered from this **intolerance**. Prejudice grew against anyone seen as an outsider. This included Jewish and Catholic people and African Americans. New laws slowed immigration to keep foreigners out.

Asiatic Barred Zone
Immigration Act of 1917

Asiatic Barred Zone
Modern International Borders

Anyone opposed to the war was viewed with suspicion. They faced threats, harassment, and violence.

Carl Schurz (1829-1906) was born in Germany. He became a U.S. Senator in Missouri and later U.S. Secretary of the Interior.

GERMANS IN AMERICA

German immigrants made up a large part of America at the start of World War I. Almost 10 percent of the population was from Germany or had parents from Germany. About 25 percent of high school students studied German in school.

James Hay (1856-1931) was chairman of the House Committee on Military Affairs.

The war had been raging for almost three years by the time America joined the fight. The U.S. government needed weapons, uniforms, and food. New government agencies took control of the **economy**. The Food Administration encouraged more food production. It assured a fair distribution between the American people, the military, and the Allies. The government controlled the railroads. It controlled the price of fuel and products needed for the war, such as iron and rubber.

Soldiers head to training camp by train in 1917.

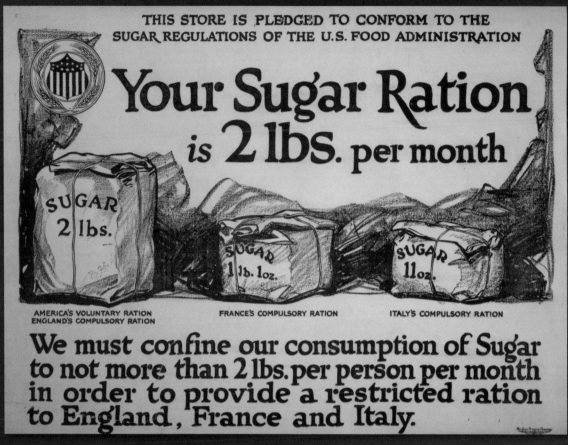

A poster lets people know they will be limited in how much sugar they can buy.

GIVE IT UP!

*During the war, sugar was rationed. That meant people could only get limited amounts. They were asked to give up other foods some of the time. For example, Americans were asked to skip meat on Meatless Mondays. This saved supplies for the **troops**.*

CHAPTER THREE

LIFE AT HOME IN WARTIME

With so many men at war, more jobs opened up at home. People found work more easily and earned better money. However, prices also rose, and taxes increased to pay for the war. The cost of the war to America ran to billions of dollars.

With more men at war, women took on jobs traditionally done by men.

To help pay for the war, the U.S. Treasury released Liberty Bonds. People bought these bonds, showing their support for the war. The government got the money as a loan. Eventually the government would pay back the money, plus a little more.

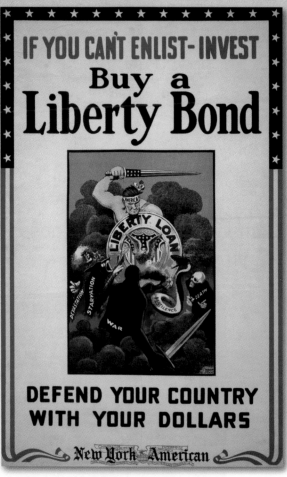

A poster encourages people to buy Liberty Bonds.

Charlie Chaplin
(1889 - 1977)

THE SILENT TREATMENT

Silent film star Charlie Chaplin urged people to buy war bonds. The bonds raised more than 20 billion dollars for the war effort. Other famous actors supported the war movement as well.

Women could not be drafted as soldiers. Still, thousands of women joined the armed forces. More than 20,000 served as nurses with the Army or Navy. The Army Medical Corps employed 2,000 female physical and occupational therapists. About 12,000 women worked in office jobs or in military intelligence.

Women at a training camp learn new skills.

The American Red Cross Motor Corps was made up entirely of women. More than 12,000 women drove ambulances for the Corps during the war.

READY TO FIGHT

Other women focused on defense at home. They joined groups that practiced military training. Some wanted to create female Army units. However, the U.S. military would not allow women into every combat job until 2016.

Women work in a factory making military supplies.

Thousands more women volunteered with organizations such as the Red Cross. Some women worked in hospitals in Europe. Others rolled bandages or knitted socks to send to the soldiers. Most groups were **segregated**. Japanese-American, Mexican-American, African-American, and Jewish women all worked separately.

WOMEN AT PEACE

Women who protested the war faced prison and violence. That didn't stop the pacifists. The Woman's Peace Party was founded in response to World War I. The organization continues today as the Women's International League for Peace and Freedom.

Members of the Woman's Peace Party.

Girls deliver blocks of ice.

With many young men away, more women began to take jobs outside the home. They worked in factories, on farms, and in all sorts of businesses. Women also practiced leadership in clubs focused on charity work. Some served on government committees. People got used to seeing women in the workforce and even in power. Women broke gender stereotypes and new roles opened for them.

An American Red Cross worker writes a letter for a wounded American soldier.

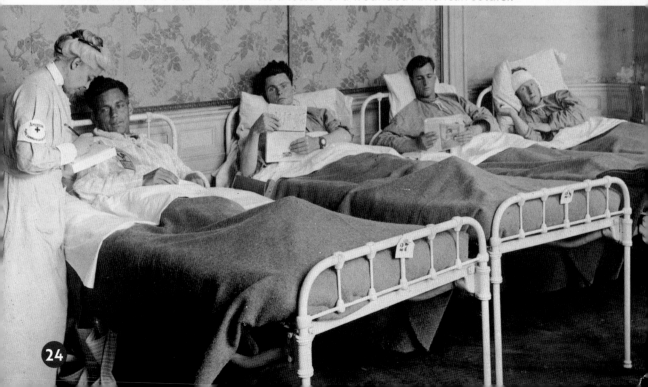

Women work in an airplane factory.

We Can Do It!

WAR PRODUCTION CO-ORDINATING COMMITTEE

LET US VOTE!

Before 1920, only a few states let women vote. During the war, women showed their skills at jobs, in volunteer organizations, and in the government. In 1920, the 19th Amendment guaranteed women the right to vote.

A family from the South arrives in Chicago.

Some African-American women worked in factories.

At the start of the war, most African Americans lived in the South. They faced political and social oppression that kept them in poverty. When America joined the war, factories in the North needed extra workers. African Americans could earn more money with better working conditions. Between 1914 and 1920, about a million African Americans moved from the South to the North.

Men found work in city factories. Most women were limited to cleaning jobs, but some worked in factories or offices.

PUT THEM IN CHARGE!

Twelve factories hired African-American women as supervisors during the war. "Their black employees had demanded it of them," a report said.

African Americans still faced **discrimination**, segregation, and even racist violence. Still, life in the North offered new freedoms. They also found new chances for political activism.

The war offered more opportunities for African-American women to work in offices.

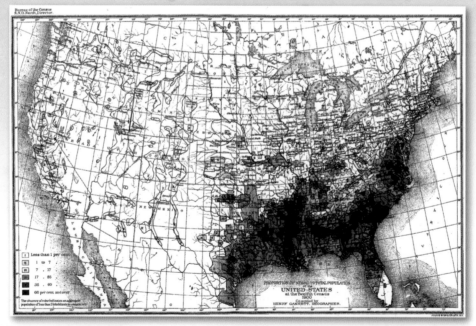

MOVING OUT

In 1910, 80 to 90 percent of African Americans lived in the South. Over the next 60 years, more than six million left. They migrated to the Northeast, Midwest, and West. By 1970, only about 40 percent of African Americans lived in the South. This movement is called the Great Migration.

Some African Americans resisted going to war. President Wilson claimed the war was a fight for democracy. How could the country fight for democracy in Europe when people did not have equal rights at home? Others saw the war as a chance to promote civil rights. They could prove their patriotism by defending their country. Then maybe African Americans could bring true democracy to the United States. About 370,000 African-American men joined the Army. More than 200,000 served in France.

Musician and band leader Louis Armstrong (1901-1971) was a major figure in jazz. He was too young to serve in WWI.

HEROES AND MUSICIANS

About 40,000 African-American troops saw battle. They served under French command. One regiment, the Harlem Hellfighters, became famous as a fighting unit and returned to America as national heroes. They were also famous for their band, which made jazz music popular in France.

The 369th Infantry was made up entirely of African-American soldiers. Nicknamed The Harlem Hellfighters, they earned a French award for their heroic actions.

GETTING ACTIVE

Many African-American women joined clubs to support the war effort. They grew politically active in other ways as well. The National Association of Colored Women (NACW) demanded voting rights for African-American women.

African-American soldiers dig a ditch.

African Americans served in two combat divisions segregated by race. Most did manual labor, such as digging ditches, cleaning toilets, and burying bodies. They often had worse housing, clothing, and services. Still, some received better healthcare and education than they'd had at home. They also had a chance to meet African soldiers serving in the French military. Education and training gave African Americans new skills. Travel gave them a broader view of the world and their race. Many would not accept a return to what they'd known before.

An African-American private from World War I.

The Harlem Hellfighters return home.

WE RETURN FIGHTING

African Americans returned home hoping for change. W. E. B. Du Bois, a leading writer and activist, wrote, "We return from fighting. We return fighting. Make way for democracy!" Marches honored the returning African-American soldiers. However, violence against them also increased. Decades passed before they achieved some of their civil rights goals.

W. E. B. Du Bois
(1868-1963)

CHAPTER FOUR

BENEFITS OF WAR?

War does not happen without great losses. Worldwide, almost 10 million soldiers died. Millions more were wounded.

Soldiers search for the dead.

At the start of the war, wounded soldiers often could not reach hospitals. A U.S. ambassador called on friends with cars to rescue the injured. This led to the start of the ambulance corps.

Red Cross ambulance drivers stand with a patient.

Wounded soldiers walk to a first-aid station.

Philanthropists and civic groups in the U.S. bought cars to be donated as ambulances. Hundreds of American university students volunteered as ambulance drivers in Europe. They got involved long before the U.S. officially joined the war.

British wartime ambulance

DEATH AND DISEASE

More than 100,000 members of the U.S. Armed Forces died during the war. More died from diseases than in battle. About 40,000 died from pneumonia near the end of the war. More than 200,000 American soldiers were wounded but lived.

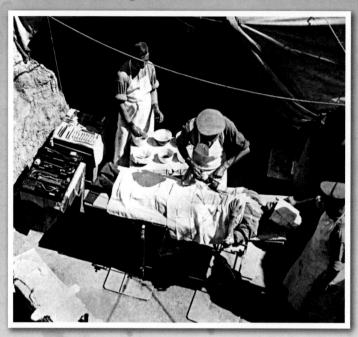

A patient is operated on at a field station in Gallipoli, Turkey.

At the beginning of the war, injured limbs were almost always cut off. Thousands of soldiers lost arms and legs, sometimes after minor injuries. Limbs were removed to prevent infections from killing the patients. The development of antiseptic to clean wounds saved many limbs and lives.

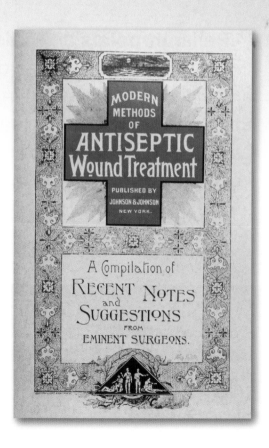

Doctors also improved surgery techniques during the war. Anesthesia made operations easier on the patient and the surgeon. A Cleveland nurse developed an anesthesia that put patients to sleep without hurting them. Medical advances such as these improved lives throughout the twentieth century.

The development of anesthesia made surgery more comfortable.

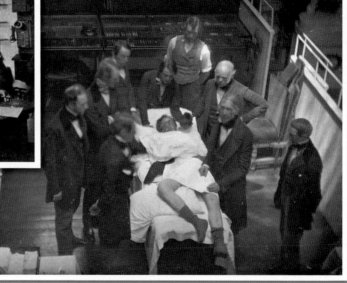

Mary M. Crawford (1884 - 1972) and a patient in 1915.

A TERRIBLE BENEFIT

The weaponry of World War I produced devastating injuries. Doctors and nurses had to quickly figure out how to treat various conditions. Blood transfusions, x-rays, and the beginnings of modern-day plastic surgery began during World War I.

Doctor Mary Merritt Crawford served at the American Hospital in France during the war. She said, "A war benefits medicine more than it benefits anybody else. It's terrible, of course, but it does."

CHAPTER FIVE

PEACE AT LAST

By the time America joined the war, both sides were exhausted by years of battle. New U.S. troops refreshed the Allies and changed the course of the war. After losing a series of battles, the Germans realized they had to end the fighting. They agreed to an armistice, or truce.

A photograph taken after German leaders signed a peace treaty.

President Wilson had developed a plan for peace. He wanted to end the war, and also secure peace and justice in the future. His plan was the basis for the **treaty** that ended the war. Not all of his ideas were adopted. Still, the world was weary of war, and public opinion favored the treaty.

Crowds celebrate the end of war.

The peace treaty included a plan to form a League of Nations. This group would help solve international disputes. President Wilson believed such a league would prevent future wars, and the U.S. public was in favor of it. However, some U.S. politicians felt it gave America's war powers to the League. Instead, the U.S. government signed a separate treaty with Germany. The U.S. never joined the League of Nations.

The League of Nations officially opened in 1920.

UNITING NATIONS

The League of Nations ended when it failed to prevent the Second World War. The United Nations came about during World War II. It also promotes international cooperation and peace. Representatives of 51 countries, including the United States, joined in 1945.

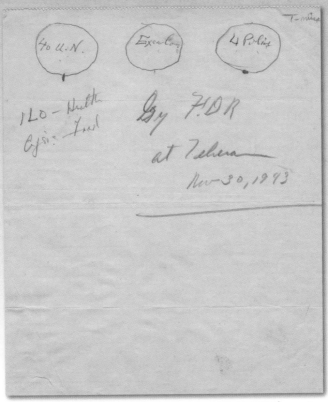

U.S. President Franklin D. Roosevelt (1882-1945) made this sketch. It shows his vision for the three branches of the United Nations.

YOU'LL PAY!

The peace agreement said Germany had to pay money to the Allies. The amount was equal to 32 billion U.S. dollars. Germany, nearly destroyed after years of war, resented these demands. The harsh conditions contributed to the rise of Hitler and World War II.

Americans celebrated the end of war, but the effects would last for some time. Isolationist feelings returned among people tired of loss and hardship. Warren G. Harding ran for president with the promise of a "return to normalcy." He won by a landslide, in the first election in which American women could vote. Harding announced that the U.S. would avoid European affairs.

Warren G. Harding (1865 – 1923) served as U.S. president from March 4, 1921, until his death in 1923.

The Nineteenth Amendment passed in 1920. It gave American women the right to vote. More than 8 million women voted in the presidential election that year.

A gathering of the Ku Klux Klan in the early 1920s.

RACISM ON THE RISE

The 1920s saw a rise in membership for the racist Ku Klux Klan. Millions of people joined. They resented social changes such as the Great Migration and the growing popularity of African-American culture. Many whites saw the Klan as supporting their traditional place at the top of society.

Not everyone wanted to return to the old ways, however. Women and African Americans, among others, had enjoyed the changes brought on by war. They wanted even more change. This led to a backlash from people who feared women and minorities gaining power.

CHAPTER SIX

LINGERING EFFECTS

After the war, the economy prospered. The 1920s were generally a time of optimism and growing wealth. Chain stores opened branches across the country. Nationwide advertising persuaded people to buy the same goods everywhere.

People listen to a radio in the mid-1920s.

The spread of radio meant everyone could listen to the same music. Musical trends such as jazz spread much more quickly with radio and the ability to record music. The telephone connected people across distances. Cars were more affordable so most families bought one, which made for easier travel. American culture became more similar across the country.

A man puts fuel in his car at a gas station in 1920.

Louise Brooks (1906 – 1985) was an American film actress and dancer. She helped popularize the flapper style.

THE NEW WOMAN

Millions of women continued working after the war. New technologies such as vacuum cleaners and washing machines meant less work at home. The flapper became the symbol of the 1920s. These young women cut their hair short and wore short skirts. They embraced the modern era.

F. Scott Fitzgerald
(1896 – 1940)

While many Americans simply wanted to forget the war, others could not. Some people questioned the values of Western civilization. How could countries that had caused such death and misery be called civilized? Artists and writers created work expressing doubt and distrust. Novels such as F. Scott Fitzgerald's *The Great Gatsby* explored corruption and excess.

Crowds flock to the opening night of a new movie.

Young people who came of age during the war and the 1920s were called the Lost Generation. "Lost" referred to feeling confused and without direction.

By the end of World War I, America had become a true world power for the first time. America was tied to other countries through politics and trade. Most Americans did not want to be involved in foreign affairs. Yet the country could no longer avoid being part of the larger world.

Many changes from the war continue to this day. Young men must register for the Selective Service and may be drafted in times of war. More women have joined the workforce and gained political power. People still argue about immigration, the power of government, and civil rights.

People prepare for a protest demonstration.

People question the government's limits on civil freedoms in times of danger. We know that a single person can change the world, for the worse or for the better.

CREATING CULTURE

As the Great Migration continued, African Americans created communities of their own within larger cities. Their experiences led to an artistic movement known as the Harlem Renaissance. The movement is named after its birthplace of Harlem in New York City.

GLOSSARY

combat (KOM-bat): fighting, especially against an enemy during a war

discrimination (dih-skri-mih-NAY-shen): the act of treating some people worse than others

economy (ih-KA-nuh-mi): the system of making and spending money

intolerance (in-TA-luh-rens): not willing to accept different people or beliefs

neutral (NU-trul): not taking a side in an argument

pacifists (PAE-sih-fihsts): people who oppose war and violence of any kind

patriotic (PAY-tri-AH-tihk): feeling love for and loyalty to one's country

philanthropists (fih-LAN-thru-pihsts): people who give money or other aid to those in need

segregated (SE-gre-GAY-ted): separated from others in a group

treaty (TREE-ti): a formal agreement between countries

troops (TRUPES): soldiers

INDEX

SHOW WHAT YOU KNOW

1. Why did America refuse to get involved in World War I at first?
2. Why did America finally join the war?
3. How did posters and ads encourage people to support the war?
4. How did the war change the role of women in American society?
5. How did the war affect African Americans?

FURTHER READING

Deary, Terry, *Frightful First World War (Horrible Histories)*, Scholastic, 2016.

Grant, R.G., *World War I: The Definitive Visual History*, DK, 2014.

Morpurgo, Michael, illustrated by Ian Beck, *Only Remembered*, Jonathan Cape, 2014.

ABOUT THE AUTHOR

M. M. Eboch writes fiction and nonfiction for all ages, but historical novels are her favorite. Her books for young people include *An Artful Escape, Walking the Dragon's Back,* and *The Well of Sacrifice.* She lives in New Mexico with her husband and their two ferrets.

www.rourkeeducationalmedia.com

Photo Credits: shutterstock.com, Wikipedia CC-Share Alike 2.0, 3.0, International. Cover: Courtesy of the Library of Congress; PG4-5; Achille Beltrame, Courtesy Library of Congress-Public Domain. PG6-7; Courtesy Library Of Congress-Public Domain, Courtesy National Archives-Public Domain. PG8-9; Courtesy Library Of Congress-Public Domain, Bundesarchiv, DVM 10 Bild-23-61-17 / CC-BY-SA 3.0. PG10-11; Courtesy National Archives-Public Domain. PG12-13; Arthur N. Edrop, George Grantham Bain, Courtesy Library of Congress-Public Domain. PG14-15; Norman Lindsay, Courtesy Library Of Congress-Public Domain. PG16-17; M.B. Brady, Courtesy National Archives-Public Domain. PG18-19; Courtesy National Archives-Public Domain. PG20-21; Winsor McCay, US.MIL. PG22-23; US.MIL, Courtesy Library Of Congress-Public Domain. PG24-25; US Red Cross-Public Domain, Courtesy Library Of Congress-Public Domain. 26-27; SCHOMBURG CENTER FOR RESEARCH IN BLACK CULTURE, PHOTOGRAPHS AND PRINTS DIVISION. PG28-29; Library Of Congress-Public Domain. PG30-31; Thompson, Paul, US.mil, Courtesy National Archives-Public Domain. PG32-33; Ernest Brooks, US Red Cross-Public Domain, Courtesy National Archives. PG34-35; Courtesy National Archives. PG36-37; DurkTalsma. PG38-39; Courtesy Library Of Congress-Public Domain. PG40-41; Everett Historical-shutterstock.com, Courtesy National Archives. PG42-43;Everett Historical-shutterstock.com, Louise Brooks, Courtesy Library Of Congress-Public Domain. PG44-45; The World's Work. PG46-47; Everett Historical-shutterstock.com, Library of Congress.

Edited by: Keli Sipperley

Produced by Blue Door Education for Rourke Educational Media. Cover and Interior design by: Jennifer Dydyk

Living Through World War I / M. M. Eboch
(American Culture and Conflict)
  ISBN 978-1-64156-416-8 (hard cover)
  ISBN 978-1-64156-542-4 (soft cover)
  ISBN 978-1-64156-665-0 (e-Book)
Library of Congress Control Number: 2018930436

Rourke Educational Media

Printed in the United States of America, North Mankato, Minnesota